ONE HUNDRED AND ONE

Classic
Love Poems

ONE HUNDRED AND ONE

Classic
Love Poems

Contemporary Books

Chicago   New York   San Francisco   Lisbon   London   Madrid   Mexico City
Milan   New Delhi   San Juan   Seoul   Singapore   Sydney   Toronto

The *McGraw-Hill* Companies

Library of Congress Cataloging-in-Publication Data

101 classic love poems.
       p.   cm.
   Includes index.
   ISBN 0-07-141929-2
   1. Love poetry.   I. Contemporary Books, Inc.   II. Title: One
hundred one classic love poems.   III. Title: One hundred and one
classic love poems.

   PN6110.L6A14   1988
   808.81'9354—dc19
                                  88-15283
                                  CIP

  2 3 4 5 6 7 8 9 0   LBM/LBM   2 1 0 9 8 7 6 5 4

ISBN 0-07-141929-2

This collection was compiled by Sara L. Whittier

McGraw-Hill books are available at special quantity discounts to use as
premiums and sales promotions, or for use in corporate training programs. For
more information, please write to the Director of Special Sales, Professional
Publishing, McGraw-Hill, Two Penn Plaza, New York, NY 10121-2298. Or
contact your local bookstore.

This book is printed on acid-free paper.

One Hundred and One Classic Love Poems

The Passionate Shepherd
to His Love

CHRISTOPHER MARLOWE
(1564–1593)

Come live with me and be my love,
And we will all the pleasures prove,
That valleys, groves, hills and fields,
Woods or steepy mountains yields.

And we will sit upon the rocks,
Seeing the shepherds feed their flocks
By shallow rivers, to whose falls
Melodious birds sing madrigals.

And I will make thee beds of roses,
And a thousand fragrant posies,
A cap of flowers and a kirtle
Embroidered all with leaves of myrtle;

A gown made of the finest wool,
Which from our pretty lambs we pull;
Fair-lined slippers for the cold,
With buckles of the purest gold;

A belt of straw and ivy buds,
With coral clasps and amber studs;
And if these pleasures may thee move,
Come live with me and be my love.

The shepherd swains shall dance and sing
For thy delight each May morning;
If these delights thy mind may move,
Then live with me and be my love.

Of My First Love

Hugh MacDiarmid
(1892–1978)

O my first love! You are in my life forever
Like the *Eas-Coul-aulin* in Sutherlandshire
Where the Amhainnan Loch Bhig burn
Plunges over the desolate slopes of Leitir Dubh.
Silhouetted against grim black rocks
This foaming mountain torrent
With its source in desolate tarns
Is savage in the extreme
As its waters with one wild leap
Hurl over the dizzy brink
Of the perpendicular cliff-face
In that great den of nature,
To be churned into spray
In the steaming depths below.
Near its base the fall splits up
Into cascades spreading out like a fan.
A legend tells how a beautiful maiden
In desperation threw herself
Over the cataract—the waters
Immediately took on the shape
Of her waving hair,
And on moonlight nights she is still to be seen
Lying near the base of the fall,
Gazing up at the tremendous cascade
Of some six hundred feet!
O my first love! Even so you lie
Near the base of my precipitous, ever lonelier and
    colder life
With your fair hair still rippling out
As I remember it between my fingers
When you let me unloosen first
(Over thirty chaotic years ago!)
That golden tumult forever!

Shall I Compare Thee to a Summer's Day?

William Shakespeare
(1564–1616)

Shall I compare thee to a summer's day?
Thou art more lovely and more temperate:
Rough winds do shake the darling buds of May,
And summer's lease hath all too short a date:
Sometime too hot the eye of heaven shines,
And often is his gold complexion dimm'd;
And every fair from fair sometime declines,
By chance, or nature's changing course untrimm'd;
But thy eternal summer shall not fade,
Nor lose possession of that fair thou ow'st,
Nor shall death brag thou wander'st in his shade,
When in eternal lines to time thou grow'st,
    So long as men can breathe, or eyes can see,
    So long lives this, and this gives life to thee.

The Silken Tent

ROBERT FROST
(1875–1963)

She is as in a field a silken tent
At midday when a sunny summer breeze
Has dried the dew and all its ropes relent,
So that in guys[1] it gently sways at ease,
And its supporting central cedar pole,
That is its pinnacle to heavenward
And signifies the sureness of the soul,
Seems to owe naught to any single cord,
But strictly held by none, is loosely bound
By countless silken ties of love and thought
To everything on earth the compass round,
And only by one's going slightly taut
In the capriciousness of summer air
Is of the slightest bondage made aware.

---

[1]ropes

4

On the Balcony

D. H. LAWRENCE
(1885–1930)

In front of the sombre mountains, a faint, lost ribbon
     of rainbow;
And between us and it, the thunder;
And down below in the green wheat, the labourers
Stand like dark stumps, still in the green wheat.

You are near to me, and your naked feet in their
     sandals,
And through the scent of the balcony's naked timber
I distinguish the scent of your hair: so now the
     limber
Lightning falls from heaven.

Adown the pale-green glacier river floats
A dark boat through the gloom—and whither?
The thunder roars. But still we have each other!
The naked lightnings in the heavens dither
And disappear—what have we but each other?
The boat has gone.

Amaturus
WILLIAM JOHNSON CORY
(1823–1892)

Somewhere beneath the sun,
　　These quivering heart-strings prove it,
Somewhere there must be one
　　Made for this soul, to move it;
Some one that hides her sweetness
　　From neighbours whom she slights,
Nor can attain completeness,
　　Nor give her heart its rights;
Some one whom I could court
　　With no great change of manner,
Still holding reason's fort,
　　Though waving fancy's banner;
A lady, not so queenly
　　As to disdain my hand,
Yet born to smile serenely
　　Like those that rule the land;
Noble, but not too proud;
　　With soft hair simply folded,
And bright face crescent-browed,
　　And throat by Muses moulded;
And eyelids lightly falling
　　On little glistening seas,
Deep-calm, when gales are brawling,
　　Though stirred by every breeze:
Swift voice, like flight of dove
　　Through minster arches floating,
With sudden turns, when love
　　Gets overnear to doting;
Keen lips, that shape soft sayings
　　Like crystals of the snow,

With pretty half-betrayings
    Of things one may not know;
Fair hand, whose touches thrill,
    Like golden rod of wonder,
Which Hermes wields at will
    Spirit and flesh to sunder;
Light foot, to press the stirrup
    In fearlessness and glee,
Or dance, till finches chirrup,
    And stars sink to the sea.

Forth, Love, and find this maid,
    Wherever she be hidden:
Speak, Love, be not afraid,
    But plead as thou art bidden;
And say, that he who taught thee
    His yearning want and pain,
Too dearly, dearly bought thee
    To part with thee in vain.

The River-Merchant's Wife: a Letter

LI T'AI-PO

(701–762)

While my hair was still cut straight across my
    forehead
I played about the front gate, pulling flowers.
You came by on bamboo stilts, playing horse,
You walked about my seat, playing with blue plums.
And we went on living in the village of Chokan:
Two small people, without dislike or suspicion.

At fourteen I married My Lord you.
I never laughed, being bashful.
Lowering my head, I looked at the wall.
Called to, a thousand times, I never looked back.

At fifteen I stopped scowling,
I desired my dust to be mingled with yours
Forever and forever and forever.
Why should I climb the lookout?

At sixteen you departed,
You went into far Ku-to-yen, by the river of swirling
    eddies,
And you have been gone five months.
The monkeys make sorrowful noise overhead.
You dragged your feet when you went out.
By the gate now, the moss is grown, the different
    mosses,
Too deep to clear them away!

The leaves fall early this autumn, in wind.
The paired butterflies are already yellow with August
Over the grass in the West garden;
They hurt me. I grow older.
If you are coming down through the narrows of the
    river Kiang,
Please let me know beforehand,
And I will come out to meet you
                        As far as Cho-fu-Sa.

Translated by Ezra Pound

Bright Star
JOHN KEATS
(1795–1821)

Bright star, would I were steadfast as thou art—
    Not in lone splendour hung aloft the night
And watching, with eternal lids apart,
    Like nature's patient, sleepless Eremite,
The moving waters at their priestlike task
    Of pure ablution round earth's human shores,
Or gazing on the new soft fallen mask
    Of snow upon the mountains and the moors—
No—yet still steadfast, still unchangeable,
    Pillow'd upon my fair love's ripening breast,
To feel for ever its soft fall and swell,
    Awake for ever in a sweet unrest,
Still, still to hear her tender-taken breath,
And so live ever—or else swoon to death.

Lullaby

W. H. AUDEN
(1907–1973)

Lay your sleeping head, my love,
Human on my faithless arm;
Time and fevers burn away
Individual beauty from
Thoughtful children, and the grave
Proves the child ephemeral:
But in my arms till break of day
Let the living creature lie,
Mortal, guilty, but to me
The entirely beautiful.

Soul and body have no bounds:
To lovers as they lie upon
Her tolerant enchanted slope
In their ordinary swoon,
Grave the vision Venus sends
Of supernatural sympathy,
Universal love and hope;
While an abstract insight wakes
Among the glaciers and the rocks
The hermit's sensual ecstasy.

Certainty, fidelity
On the stroke of midnight pass
Like vibrations of a bell,
And fashionable madmen raise
Their pedantic boring cry:
Every farthing of the cost,
All the dreaded cards foretell,
Shall be paid, but from this night
Not a whisper, not a thought,
Not a kiss nor look be lost.

Beauty, midnight, vision dies:
Let the winds of dawn that blow
Softly round your dreaming head
Such a day of sweetness show
Eye and knocking heart may bless,
Find the mortal world enough;
Noons of dryness see you fed
By the involuntary powers,
Nights of insult let you pass
Watched by every human love.

The Night-Piece: To Julia

ROBERT HERRICK

(1591–1674)

Her eyes the glow-worm lend thee;
The shooting stars attend thee;
 And the elves also,
 Whose little eyes glow
Like the sparks of fire, befriend thee.

No will-o'-th'-wisp mislight thee,
Nor snake or slow-worm bite thee;
 But on, on thy way,
 Not making a stay,
Since ghost there's none to affright thee.

Let not the dark thee cumber;
What though the moon does slumber?
 The stars of the night
 Will lend thee their light
Like tapers clear, without number.

Then, Julia, let me woo thee,
Thus, thus, to come unto me;
 And when I shall meet
 Thy silvery feet,
My soul I'll pour into thee.

Love's Philosophy

PERCY BYSSHE SHELLEY
(1792–1822)

The fountains mingle with the river,
  And the rivers with the ocean;
The winds of heaven mix forever,
  With a sweet emotion;
Nothing in the world is single;
  All things by a law divine
In one another's being mingle:—
  Why not I with thine?

See! the mountains kiss high heaven,
  And the waves clasp one another;
No sister flower would be forgiven
  If it disdained its brother;
And the sunlight clasps the earth,
  And the moonbeams kiss the sea:—
What are all these kissings worth,
  If thou kiss not me?

Two in the Campagna

ROBERT BROWNING

(1812–1889)

I wonder do you feel to-day
   As I have felt since, hand in hand,
We sat down on the grass, to stray
   In spirit better through the land,
This morn of Rome and May?

For me, I touched a thought, I know,
   Has tantalized me many times,
(Like turns of thread the spiders throw
   Mocking across our path) for rhymes
To catch at and let go.

Help me to hold it! First it left
   The yellowing fennel, run to seed
There, branching from the brickwork's cleft,
   Some old tomb's ruin: yonder weed
Took up the floating weft,

Where one small orange cup amassed
   Five beetles,—blind and green they grope
Among the honey-meal: and last,
   Everywhere on the grassy slope
I traced it. Hold it fast!

The champaign with its endless fleece
   Of feathery grasses everywhere!
Silence and passion, joy and peace,
   An everlasting wash of air—
Rome's ghost since her decease.

Such life here, through such lengths of hours,
   Such miracles performed in play,
Such primal naked forms of flowers,

14

Such letting nature have her way
While heaven looks from its towers!

How say you? Let us, O my dove,
    Let us be unashamed of soul,
As earth lies bare to heaven above!
    How is it under our control
To love or not to love?

I would that you were all to me,
    You that are just so much, no more.
Nor yours nor mine, nor slave nor free!
    Where does the fault lie? What the core
O' the wound, since wound must be?

I would I could adopt your will,
    See with your eyes, and set my heart
Beating by yours, and drink my fill
    At your soul's springs,—your part my part
In life, for good and ill.

No. I yearn upward, touch you close,
    Then stand away. I kiss your cheek,
Catch your soul's warmth,—I pluck the rose
    And love it more than tongue can speak—
Then the good minute goes.

Already how am I so far
    Out of that minute? Must I go
Still like the thistle-ball, no bar,
    Onward, whenever light winds blow,
Fixed by no friendly star?

Just when I seemed about to learn!
    Where is the thread now? Off again!
The old trick! Only I discern—
    Infinite passion, and the pain
Of finite hearts that yearn.

Upon Julia's Clothes
ROBERT HERRICK
(1591–1674)

Whenas in silks my Julia goes,
Then, then, methinks, how sweetly flows
That liquefaction of her clothes.

Next, when I cast mine eyes, and see
That brave vibration, each way free,
O, how that glittering taketh me!

To His Coy Mistress
ANDREW MARVELL
(1621–1678)

Had we but world enough, and time,
This coyness, lady, were no crime.
We would sit down, and think which way
To walk, and pass our long love's day.
Thou by the Indian Ganges' side
Shouldst rubies find: I by the tide
Of Humber would complain. I would
Love you ten years before the flood,
And you should, if you please, refuse
Till the conversion of the Jews;
My vegetable love should grow
Vaster than empires and more slow;
An hundred years should go to praise
Thine eyes, and on thy forehead gaze;
Two hundred to adore each breast,
But thirty thousand to the rest;

An age at least to every part,
And the last age should show your heart.
For, lady, you deserve this state,
Nor would I love at lower rate.

But at my back I always hear
Time's wingèd chariot hurrying near,
And yonder all before us lie
Deserts of vast eternity.
Thy beauty shall no more be found,
Nor, in thy marble vault, shall sound
My echoing song; then worms shall try
That long-preserved virginity,
And your quaint honor turn to dust,
And into ashes all my lust:
The grave's a fine and private place,
But none, I think, do there embrace.

Now, therefore, while the youthful hue
Sits on thy skin like morning dew,
And while thy willing soul transpires
At every pore with instant fires,
Now let us sport us while we may,
And now, like amorous birds of prey,
Rather at once our time devour,
Than languish in his slow-chapped power.
Let us roll all our strength and all
Our sweetness up into one ball,
And tear our pleasures with rough strife
Thorough the iron gates of life;
Thus, though we cannot make our sun
Stand still, yet we will make him run.

Rubaiyat

OMAR KHAYYÁM

(?-1123)

*These are five of the most well-known sections of this
famous Persian poem, which is 101 stanzas long.*

A Book of Verses underneath the Bough,
A Jug of Wine, a Loaf of Bread—and Thou
    Beside me singing in the Wilderness—
Oh, Wilderness were Paradise enow!

. . . . .

Ah, make the most of what we yet may spend,
Before we too into the Dust descend;
    Dust into Dust, and under Dust to lie,
Sans Wine, sans Song, sans Singer, and—sans End!

. . . . .

The Moving Finger writes; and, having writ,
Moves on: nor all your Piety nor Wit
    Shall lure it back to cancel half a Line,
Nor all your Tears wash out a Word of it.

. . . . .

Yet Ah, that Spring should vanish with the Rose!
That Youth's sweet-scented manuscript should close!
    The Nightingale that in the branches sang,
Ah whence, and whither flown again, who knows!

. . . . .

Ah Love! could you and I with Him conspire
To grasp this sorry Scheme of Things Entire,
    Would not we shatter it to bits—and then
Re-mold it nearer to the Heart's Desire!

Translated by Edward FitzGerald

Come, My Celia

BEN JONSON
(1573–1637)

Come, my Celia, let us prove,
While we can, the sports of love.
Time will not be ours for ever;
He, at length, our good will sever.
Spend not then his gifts in vain:
Suns that set may rise again.
But if once we lose this light,
'Tis with us perpetual night.
Why should we defer our joys?
Fame and rumor are but toys.
Cannot we delude the eyes
Of a few poor household spies?
Or his easier ears beguile,
Thus removéd by our wile?
'Tis no sin love's fruits to steal,
But the sweet thefts to reveal;
To be taken, to be seen,
These have crimes accounted been.

The Little Old Lady in Lavender Silk

DOROTHY PARKER
(1893–1967)

I was seventy-seven, come August,
  I shall shortly be losing my bloom;
I've experienced zephyr and raw gust
  and (symbolical) flood and simoom.

When you come to this time of abatement,
  To this passing from Summer to Fall,
It is manners to issue a statement
  As to what you got out of it all.

So I'll say, though reflection unnerves me
  And pronouncements I dodge as I can,
That I think (if my memory serves me)
  There was nothing more fun than a man!

In my youth, when the crescent was too wan
  To embarrass with beams from above,
By the aid of some local Don Juan
  I fell into the habit of love.

And I learned how to kiss and be merry—an
  Education left better unsung.
My neglect of the waters Pierian
  Was a scandal when Grandma was young.

Though the shabby unbalanced the splendid,
    And the bitter outmeasured the sweet,
I should certainly do as I then did,
    Were I given the chance to repeat.

For contrition is hollow and wraithful,
    And regret is no part of my plan,
And I think (if my memory's faithful)
    There was nothing more fun than a man!

From *Twelfth Night*
WILLIAM SHAKESPEARE
(1564–1616)

O mistress mine, where are you roaming?
O, stay and hear, your true love's coming,
    That can sing both high and low:
Trip no further, pretty sweeting,
Journeys end in lovers meeting,
    Every wise man's son doth know.

What is love? 'Tis not hereafter;
Present mirth hath present laughter;
    What's to come is still unsure:
In delay there lies no plenty;
Then come kiss me, sweet and twenty,
    Youth's a stuff will not endure.

When I Was One-And-Twenty

A. E. HOUSMAN
(1859–1936)

When I was one-and-twenty
  I heard a wise man say,
"Give crowns and pounds and guineas
  But not your heart away;
Give pearls away and rubies
  But keep your fancy free."
But I was one-and-twenty,
  No use to talk to me.

When I was one-and-twenty
  I heard him say again,
"The heart out of the bosom
  Was never given in vain;
'Tis paid with sighs a plenty
  And sold for endless rue."
And I am two-and-twenty,
  And oh, 'tis true, 'tis true.

Sweet Disorder

ROBERT HERRICK

(1591–1674)

A sweet disorder in the dress
Kindles in clothes a wantonness:
A lawn about the shoulders thrown
Into a fine distraction—
An erring lace, which here and there
Enthrals the crimson stomacher—
A cuff neglectful, and thereby
Ribbands to flow confusedly—
A winning wave, deserving note,
In the tempestuous petticoat—
A careless shoe-string, in whose tie
I see a wild civility—
Do more bewitch me than when art
Is too precise in every part.

Song

WILLIAM DAVENANT
(1606–1668)

The lark now leaves his watery nest,
  And climbing shakes his dewy wings.
He takes this window for the East,
  And to implore your light he sings—
Awake, awake! the morn will never rise
Till she can dress her beauty at your eyes.

The merchant bows unto the seaman's star,
  The plowman from the sun his season takes;
But still the lover wonders what they are
  Who look for day before his mistress wakes.
Awake, awake! break through your veils of lawn!
Then draw your curtains, and begin the dawn!

The Sun Rising

JOHN DONNE

(1573–1631)

Busy old fool, unruly Sun,
    Why dost thou thus,
Through windows, and through curtains call on us?
Must to thy motions lovers' seasons run?
    Saucy pedantic wretch, go chide
    Late school-boys, and sour 'prentices,
  Go tell court-huntsmen that the King will ride,
  Call country ants to harvest offices;
Love, all alike, no season knows, nor clime,
Nor hours, days, months, which are the rags of time.

Thy beams, so reverend, and strong
    Why shouldst thou think?
I could eclipse and cloud them with a wink,
But that I would not lose her sight so long:
    If her eyes have not blinded thine,
    Look, and tomorrow late, tell me,
  Whether both the Indias of spice and mine
  Be where thou left'st them, or lie here with me.
Ask for those kings whom thou saw'st yesterday,
And thou shalt hear, 'All here in one bed lay.'

She is all States, and all Princes, I;
    Nothing else is.
Princes do but play us; compar'd to this,
All honour's mimic; all wealth alchemy.
    Thou Sun art half as happy as we,
    In that the world's contracted thus;
  Thine age asks ease, and since thy duties be
  To warm the world, that's done in warming us.
Shine here to us, and thou art every where;
This bed thy centre is, these walls, thy sphere.

Song from Maud

ALFRED, LORD TENNYSON

(1809–1892)

Come into the garden, Maud,
  For the black bat, night, has flown,
Come into the garden, Maud,
  I am here at the gate alone;
And the woodbine spices are wafted abroad,
  And the musk of the rose is blown.

For a breeze of morning moves,
  And the planet of love is on high,
Beginning to faint in the light that she loves
  On a bed of daffodil sky,
To faint in the light of the sun she loves,
  To faint in his light, and to die.

All night have the roses heard
  The flute, violin, bassoon;
All night has the casement jessamine stirred
  To the dancers dancing in tune;
Till a silence fell with the waking bird,
  And a hush with the setting moon.

I said to the lily, "There is but one,
  With whom she has heart to be gay.
When will the dancers leave her alone?
  She is weary of dance and play."
Now half to the setting moon are gone,
  And half to the rising day;
Low on the sand and loud on the stone
  The last wheel echoes away.

I said to the rose, "The brief night goes
    In babble and revel and wine.
O young lord-lover, what sighs are those,
    For one that will never be thine
But mine, but mine," so I sware to the rose,
    "Forever and ever, mine."

And the soul of the rose went into my blood,
    As the music clashed in the Hall;
And long by the garden lake I stood,
    For I heard your rivulet fall
From the lake to the meadow and on to the wood,
    Our wood, that is dearer than all;

From the meadow your walks have left so sweet
    That whenever a March-wind sighs
He sets the jewel-print of your feet
    In violets blue as your eyes,
To the woody hollows in which we meet
    And the valleys of Paradise.

The slender acacia would not shake
    One long milk-bloom on the tree;
The white lake-blossom fell into the lake
    As the pimpernel dozed on the lea;
But the rose was awake all night for your sake,
    Knowing your promise to me;
The lilies and roses were all awake,
    They sighed for the dawn and thee.

Queen rose of the rosebud garden of girls,
    Come hither, the dances are done,
In gloss of satin and glimmer of pearls,
    Queen of lily and rose in one;
Shine out, little head, sunning over with curls,
    To the flowers, and be their sun.

There has fallen a splendid tear
    From the passion-flower at the gate.
She is coming, my dove, my dear;
    She is coming, my life, my fate.
The red rose cries, "She is near, she is near;"
    And the white rose weeps, "She is late;"
The larkspur listens, "I hear, I hear;"
    And the lily whispers, "I wait."

She is coming, my own, my sweet;
    Were it ever so airy a tread,
My heart would hear her and beat,
    Were it earth in an earthy bed;
My dust would hear her and beat,
    Had I lain for a century dead,
Would start and tremble under her feet,
    And blossom in purple and red.

Meeting at Night

ROBERT BROWNING
(1812–1889)

The gray sea and the long black land;
And the yellow half-moon large and low;
And the startled little waves that leap
In fiery ringlets from their sleep,
As I gain the cove with pushing prow,
And quench its speed i' the slushy sand.

Then a mile of warm sea-scented beach;
Three fields to cross till a farm appears;
A tap at the pane, the quick sharp scratch
And blue spurt of a lighted match,
And a voice less loud, through its joys and fears,
Than the two hearts beating each to each!

The Banks o' Doon

ROBERT BURNS
(1759–1796)

Ye flowery banks o' bonie Doon,
    How can ye blume sae fair?
How can ye chant, ye little birds,
    And I sae fu' o' care!

Thou'll break my heart, thou bonie bird,
    That sings upon the bough!
Thou minds me o' the happy days
    When my fause luve was true.

Thou'll break my heart, thou bonie bird,
    That sings beside thy mate.
For sae I sat, and sae I sang,
    And wist na o' my fate.

Aft hae I rov'd by bonie Doon,
    To see the woodbine twine;
And ilka bird sang o' its luve,
    And sae did I o' mine.

Wi' lightsome heart I pu'd a rose,
    Upon its thorny tree;
But my fause luver staw my rose,
    And left the thorn wi' me.

From *Sappho*

WALTER SAVAGE LANDOR
(1775–1864)

Mother, I cannot mind my wheel;
　My fingers ache, my lips are dry:
Oh! if you felt the pain I feel!
　But Oh, who ever felt as I?

No longer could I doubt him true;
　All other men may use deceit:
He always said my eyes were blue,
　And often swore my lips were sweet.

From *Idea*

MICHAEL DRAYTON
(1563–1631)

Since there's no help, come, let us kiss and part!
Nay, I have done, you get no more of me;
And I am glad, yea, glad with all my heart,
That thus so cleanly I myself can free.
Shake hands for ever, cancel all our vows;
And when we meet at any time again,
Be it not seen in either of our brows,
That we one jot of former love retain.
Now at the last gasp of Love's latest breath,
When, his pulse failing, Passion speechless lies,
When Faith is kneeling by his bed of death,
And Innocence is closing up his eyes,—
Now, if thou wouldst, when all have given him over,
From death to life thou might'st him yet recover.

Non Sum Qualis Eram Bonae Sub Regno Cynarae

ERNEST DOWSON
(1867–1900)

Last night ah, yesternight, betwixt her lips and mine
There fell thy shadow, Cynara! thy breath was shed
Upon my soul between the kisses and the wine;
And I was desolate and sick of an old passion,
   Yea, I was desolate and bowed my head:
I have been faithful to thee, Cynara! in my fashion.

All night upon mine heart I felt her warm heart beat,
Night-long within mine arms in love and sleep she
     lay;
Surely the kisses of her bought red mouth were
     sweet;
But I was desolate and sick of an old passion,
   When I awoke and found the dawn was gray:
I have been faithful to thee, Cynara! in my fashion.

I have forgot much, Cynara! gone with the wind,
Flung roses, roses riotously with the throng,
Dancing, to put thy pale, lost lilies out of mind;
But I was desolate and sick of an old passion,
   Yea, all the time, because the dance was long:
I have been faithful to thee, Cynara! in my fashion.

I cried for madder music and for stronger wine,
But when the feast is finished and the lamps expire,
Then falls thy shadow, Cynara the night is thine;
And I am desolate and sick of an old passion,
   Yea hungry for the lips of my desire:
I have been faithful to thee, Cynara in my fashion.

Oh, Think Not I Am Faithful to a Vow!

Edna St. Vincent Millay
(1892–1950)

Oh, think not I am faithful to a vow!
Faithless am I save to love's self alone.
Were you not lovely I would leave you now:
After the feet of beauty fly my own.
Were you not still my hunger's rarest food,
And water ever to my wildest thirst,
I would desert you—think not but I would!—
And seek another as I sought you first.
But you are mobile as the veering air,
And all your charms more changeful than the tide,
Wherefore to be inconstant is no care:
I have but to continue at your side.
So wanton, light and false, my love, are you,
I am most faithless when I most am true.

"And Forgive Us Our Trespasses"

Aphra Behn
(1640–1689)

*The first English woman to make her living as a profes-
sional writer, Aphra Behn lived a highly adventurous
life. She married a merchant, and in addition to writing
drama, novels, poems, and translations, she served her
country as a spy.*

How prone we are to sin; how sweet were made
The pleasures our resistless hearts invade.
Of all my crimes, the breach of all thy laws,
Love, soft bewitching love, has been the cause.
Of all the paths that vanity has trod,
That sure will soonest be forgiven by God.
If things on earth may be to heaven resembled,
It must be love, pure, constant, undissembled.
But if to sin by chance the charmer press,
Forgive, O Lord, forgive our trespasses.

To Celia

SIR CHARLES SEDLEY
(1639?–1701)

Not, Celia, that I juster am,
   Or better than the rest!
For I would change each hour like them,
   Were not my heart at rest.

But I am tied to very thee
   By every thought I have;
Thy face I only care to see,
   Thy heart I only crave.

All that in woman is adored
   In thy dear self I find;
For the whole sex can but afford
   The handsome and the kind.

Why then should I seek further store
   And still make love anew?
When change itself can give no more,
   'Tis easy to be true.

To the Virgins to Make Much of Time

ROBERT HERRICK

(1591–1674)

Gather ye rosebuds while ye may,
  Old Time is still a-flying;
And this same flower that smiles to-day,
  To-morrow will be dying.

The glorious lamp of heaven, the sun,
  The higher he's a-getting,
The sooner will his race be run,
  And nearer he's to setting

That age is best which is the first,
  When youth and blood are warmer;
But being spent, the worse and worst
  Times still succeed the former.
Then be not coy, but use your time,
  And while ye may, go marry;
For, having lost but once your prime,
  You may forever tarry.

Billy Boy

UNKNOWN

Oh, where have you been, Billy boy, Billy boy,
Oh, where have you been, charming Billy?
I have been to seek a wife, she's the joy of my young
    life,
She's a young thing and cannot leave her mother.

Did she ask you to come in, Billy boy, Billy boy,
Did she ask you to come in, charming Billy?
She did ask me to come in, with a dimple in her
    chin,
She's a young thing and cannot leave her mother.

Did she ask you to sit down, Billy boy, Billy boy,
Did she ask you to sit down, charming Billy?
She did ask me to sit down, with a curtsey to the
    ground,
She's a young thing and cannot leave her mother.

Did she set for you a chair, Billy boy, Billy boy,
Did she set for you a chair, charming Billy?
Yes, she set for me a chair, she's got ringlets in her
    hair,
She's a young thing and cannot leave her mother.

How old is she, Billy boy, Billy boy,
How old is she, charming Billy?
She's three times six, four times seven, twenty-eight
    and eleven,
She's a young thing and cannot leave her mother.

How tall is she, Billy boy, Billy boy,
How tall is she, charming Billy?
She's as tall as any pine and as straight's a pumpkin
vine,
She's a young thing and cannot leave her mother.

Can she make a cherry pie, Billy boy, Billy boy,
Can she make a cherry pie, charming Billy?
She can make a cherry pie, quick's a cat can wink her
eye,
She's a young thing and cannot leave her mother.

Does she often go to church, Billy boy, Billy boy,
Does she often go to church, charming Billy?
Yes, she often goes to church, with her bonnet white
as birch,
She's a young thing and cannot leave her mother.

Can she make a pudding well, Billy boy, Billy boy,
Can she make a pudding well, charming Billy?
She can make a pudding well, I can tell it by the
smell,
She's a young thing and cannot leave her mother.

Can she make a feather-bed, Billy boy, Billy boy,
Can she make a feather-bed, charming Billy?
She can make a feather-bed, place the pillows at the
head,
She's a young thing and cannot leave her mother.

Can she card and can she spin, Billy boy, Billy boy,
Can she card and can she spin, charming Billy?
She can card and she can spin, she can do most
anything,
She's a young thing and cannot leave her mother.

Sally in Our Alley

HENRY CAREY
(1693?–1743)

Of all the girls that are so smart
  There's none like pretty Sally;
She is the darling of my heart,
  And she lives in our alley.
There is no lady in the land
  Is half so sweet as Sally;
She is the darling of my heart,
  And she lives in our alley.

Her father he makes cabbage-nets
  And through the streets does cry 'em;
Her mother she sells laces long
  To such as please to buy 'em:
But sure such folks could ne'er beget
  So sweet a girl as Sally!
She is the darling of my heart,
  And she lives in our alley.

When she is by, I leave my work,
  I love her so sincerely;
My master comes like any Turk,
  And bangs me most severely:
But let him bang his bellyful,
  I'll bear it all for Sally;
She is the darling of my heart,
  And she lives in our alley.

Of all the days that's in the week
    I dearly love but one day—
And that's the day that comes betwixt
    A Saturday and Monday;
For then I'm drest all in my best
    To walk abroad with Sally;
She is the darling of my heart,
    And she lives in our alley.

My master carries me to church,
    And often am I blamèd
Because I leave him in the lurch
    As soon as text is namèd;
I leave the church in sermon-time
    And slink away to Sally;
She is the darling of my heart,
    And she lives in our alley.

When Christmas comes about again,
    O then I shall have money;
I'll board it up, and, box and all,
    I'll give it to my honey:
I would it were ten thousand pound,
    I'd give it all to Sally;
She is the darling of my heart,
    And she lives in our alley.

My master and the neighbors all
    Make game of me and Sally,
And, but for her, I'd better be
    A slave and row a galley;
But when my seven long years are out
    O then I'll marry Sally,—
O then we'll wed, and then we'll bed . . .
    But not in our alley!

Wish for a Young Wife

THEODORE ROETHKE
(1908-1963)

My lizard, my lively writher,
May your limbs never wither,
May the eyes in your face
Survive the green ice
Of envy's mean gaze;
May you live out your life
Without hate, without grief,
May your hair ever blaze,
In the sun, in the sun,
When I am undone,
When I am no one.

She Tells Her Love While Half Asleep

ROBERT GRAVES
(1895-1985)

She tells her love while half asleep
In the dark hours,
With half-words whispered low:
As Earth stirs in her winter sleep
And puts out grass and flowers
Despite the snow,
Despite the falling snow.

Fulfillment

WILLIAM CAVENDISH
(1592–1676)

There is no happier life
    But in a wife;
The comforts are so sweet
    When two do meet.
'Tis plenty, peace, a calm
    Like dropping balm;
Love's weather is so fair,
    Like perfumed air.
Each word such pleasure brings
    Like soft-touched strings;
Love's passion moves the heart
    On either part;
Such harmony together,
    So pleased in either.
No discords; concords still;
    Sealed with one will.
By love, God made man one,
    Yet not alone.
Like stamps of king and queen
    It may be seen:
Two figures on one coin,
    So do they join,
Only they not embrace.
    We, face to face.

Part of Plenty

BERNARD SPENCER

(1909–1963)

When she carries food to the table and stoops down
—Doing this out of love—and lays soup with its
    good
Tickling smell, or fry winking from the fire
And I look up, perhaps from a book I am reading
Or other work: there is an importance of beauty
Which can't be accounted for by there and then,
And attacks me, but not separately from the welcome
Of the food, or the grace of her arms.
When she puts a sheaf of tulips in a jug
And pours in water and presses to one side
The upright stems and leaves that you hear creak,
Or loosens them, or holds them up to show me,
So that I see the tangle of their necks and cups
With the curls of her hair, and the body they are held
Against, and the stalk of the small waist rising
And flowering in the shape of breasts;
Whether in the bringing of the flowers or of the
    food
She offers plenty, and is part of plenty,
And whether I see her stooping, or leaning with the
    flowers,
What she does is ages old, and she is not simply,
No, but lovely in that way.

Habitation
MARGARET ATWOOD
(b.1939)

Marriage is not
a house or even a tent

it is before that, and colder:

the edge of the forest, the edge
of the desert
                the unpainted stairs
at the back where we squat
outside, eating popcorn

the edge of the receding glacier

where painfully and with wonder
at having survived even
this far

we are learning to make fire

This Is Just to Say

WILLIAM CARLOS WILLIAMS
(1883–1963)

I have eaten
the plums
that were in
the icebox

and which
you were probably
saving
for breakfast

Forgive me
they were delicious
so sweet
and so cold

To My Dear and Loving Husband

ANNE BRADSTREET

(1612?–1672)

Anne Bradstreet sailed from England in 1630 as a member of one of the founding families of the Massachusetts Bay Colony. America's first poet dedicated this poem to her husband, Simon Bradstreet.

If ever two were one, then surely we.
If ever man were loved by wife, then thee;
If ever wife was happy in a man,
Compare with me, ye women, if you can.
I prize thy love more than whole mines of gold
Or all the riches that the East doth hold.
My love is such that rivers cannot quench,
Nor ought but love from thee, give recompense.
Thy love is such I can no way repay,
The heavens reward thee manifold, I pray.
Then while we live, in love let's so persevere
That when we live no more, we may live ever.

The Marriage

YVOR WINTERS

(1900-1968)

Incarnate for our marriage you appeared,
Flesh living in the spirit and endeared
By minor graces and slow sensual change.
Through every nerve we made our spirits range.
We fed our minds on every mortal thing:
The lacy fronds of carrots in the spring,
Their flesh sweet on the tongue, the salty wine
From bitter grapes, which gathered through the vine
The mineral drouth of autumn concentrate,
Wild spring in dream escaping, the debate
Of flesh and spirit on those vernal nights,
Its resolution in naive delights,
The young kids bleating softly in the rain—
All this to pass, not to return again.
And when I found your flesh did not resist,
It was the living spirit that I kissed,
It was the spirit's change in which I lay:
Thus, mind in mind we waited for the day.
When flesh shall fall away, and, falling, stand
Wrinkling with shadow over face and hand,
Still I shall meet you on the verge of dust
And know you as a faithful vestige must.
And, in commemoration of our lust,
May our heirs seal us in a single urn,
A single spirit never to return.

Sonnets from the Portuguese
ELIZABETH BARRETT BROWNING
(1806–1861)

Elizabeth Barrett was already a successful poet when she met the poet Robert Browning and embarked on a romance that became one of the world's great love stories. She began writing a series of sonnets as soon as they met, but did not share them with him until several years later. Here are four of the impassioned, intimate poems she presented to her husband as "some poems about you." They were later published under the title Sonnets from the Portuguese, *named in remembrance of Robert Browning's pet name for his dark-haired wife, "my little Portuguese."*

How Do I Love Thee?
Let Me Count the Ways

How do I love thee? Let me count the ways.
I love thee to the depth and breadth and height
My soul can reach, when feeling out of sight
For the ends of Being and ideal Grace.
I love thee to the level of everyday's
Most quiet need, by sun and candle-light.
I love thee freely, as men strive for Right;
I love thee purely, as they turn from Praise.
I love thee with the passion put to use
In my old griefs, and with my childhood's faith.
I love thee with a love I seemed to lose
With my lost saints,—I love thee with the breath,
Smiles, tears, of all my life!—and, if God choose,
I shall but love thee better after death.

When Our Two Souls Stand Up Erect and Strong

When our two souls stand up erect and strong,
Face to face, silent, drawing nigh and nigher,
Until the lengthening wings break into fire
At either curvèd point,—what bitter wrong
Can the earth do to us, that we should not long
Be here contented? Think. In mounting higher,
The angels would press us on and aspire
To drop some golden orb of perfect song
Into our deep, dear silence. Let us stay
Rather on earth, Belovèd—where the unfit
Contrarious moods of men recoil away
And isolate pure spirits, and permit
A place to stand and love in for a day,
With darkness and the death-hour rounding it.

First Time He Kissed Me, He but Only Kissed

First time he kissed me, he but only kiss'd
  The fingers of this hand wherewith I write;
  And ever since, it grew more clean and white,
Slow to world-greetings, quick with its "Oh, list,"
When the angels speak. A ring of amethyst
  I could not wear here, plainer to my sight,
  Than that first kiss. The second pass'd in height
The first, and sought the forehead, and half miss'd,
Half falling on the hair. Oh, beyond meed!
  That was the chrism of love, which love's own
      crown,
With sanctifying sweetness, did precede.
  The third upon my lips was folded down
In perfect, purple state; since when, indeed,
  I have been proud, and said, "My love, my own!"

If Thou Must Love Me, Let It Be for Nought

If thou must love me, let it be for nought
Except for love's sake only. Do not say
'I love her for her smile—her look—her way
Of speaking gently,—for a trick of thought
That falls in well with mine, and certes brought
A sense of pleasant ease on such a day'—
For these things in themselves, Belovéd, may
Be changed, or change for thee,—and love, so
    wrought,
May be unwrought so. Neither love me for
Thine own dear pity's wiping my cheeks dry,—
A creature might forget to weep, who bore
Thy comfort long, and lose thy love thereby!
But love me for love's sake, that evermore
Thou mayst love on, through love's eternity.

Now!

ROBERT BROWNING
(1812-1889)

Out of your whole life give but a moment!
  All of your life that has gone before,
  All to come after it,—so you ignore,
So you make perfect the present; condense,
In a rapture of rage, for perfection's endowment,
Thought and feeling and soul and sense,
Merged in a moment which gives me at last
You around me for once, you beneath me, above me—
Me, sure that, despite of time future, time past,
This tick of life-time's one moment you love me!
How long such suspension may linger? Ah, Sweet,
  The moment eternal—just that and no more—
  When ecstasy's utmost we clutch at the core,
While cheeks burn, arms open, eyes shut, and lips
    meet!

From *Paradise Lost*

JOHN MILTON
(1608–1674)

Here, Eve speaks to Adam.

With thee conversing I forget all time,
All seasons and their change, all please alike.
Sweet is the breath of morn, her rising sweet,
With charm of earliest birds; pleasant the sun
When first on this delightful land he spreads
His orient beams, on herb, tree, fruit, and flower,
Glistring with dew; fragrant the fertile earth
After soft showers; and sweet the coming on
Of grateful evening mild, then silent night
With this her solemn bird and this fair moon,
And these the gems of heav'n, her starry train:
But neither breath of morn when she ascends
With charm of earliest birds, nor rising sun
On this delightful land, nor herb, fruit, flower,
Glistring with dew, nor fragrance after showers,
Nor grateful evening mild, nor silent night
With this her solemn bird, nor walk by moon,
Or glittering starlight without thee is sweet.

The Ragged Wood

WILLIAM BUTLER YEATS
(1865–1939)

O hurry where by water among the trees
The delicate-stepping stag and his lady sigh,
When they have but looked upon their images—
Would none had ever loved but you and I!

Or have you heard that sliding silver-shoed
Pale silver-proud queen-woman of the sky,
When the sun looked out of his golden hood?—
O that none ever loved but you and I!

O hurry to the ragged wood, for there
I will drive all those lovers out and cry—
O my share of the world, O yellow hair!
No one has ever loved but you and I.

Song of Solomon, Chapter Two

ATTRIBUTED TO KING SOLOMON

(tenth century B.C.)

I am a rose of Sharon,
   a lily of the valleys.

As a lily among brambles,
   so is my love among maidens.

As an apple tree among the trees of the wood,
   so is my beloved among young men.
With great delight I sat in his shadow,
   and his fruit was sweet to my taste.
He brought me to the banqueting house,
   and his banner over me was love.
Sustain me with raisins,
   refresh me with apples;
   for I am sick with love.
O that his left hand were under my head,
   and that his right hand embraced me!
I adjure you, O daughters of Jerusalem,
   by the gazelles or the hinds of the field,
that you stir not up nor awaken love
   until it please.
The voice of my beloved!
   Behold, he comes,
leaping upon the mountains,
   bounding over the hills.
My beloved is like a gazelle,
   or a young stag.
Behold, there he stands
   behind our wall,
gazing in at the windows,
   looking through the lattice.

My beloved speaks and says to me:
"Arise, my love, my fair one,
   and come away;
for lo, the winter is past,
   the rain is over and gone.
The flowers appear on the earth,
   the time of singing has come,
and the voice of the turtledove
   is heard in our land.
The fig tree puts forth its figs,
   and the vines are in blossom;
   they give forth fragrance.
Arise, my love, my fair one,
   and come away.
O my dove, in the clefts of the rock,
   in the covert of the cliff,
let me see your face,
   let me hear your voice,
for your voice is sweet,
   and your face is comely.
Catch us the foxes,
   the little foxes,
that spoil the vineyards,
   for our vineyards are in blossom."

My beloved is mine and I am his,
   he pastures his flock among the lilies.
Until the day breathes
   and the shadows flee,
turn, my beloved, be like a gazelle,
   or a young stag upon rugged mountains.

Echo
CHRISTINA ROSSETTI
(1830-1894)

Come to me in the silence of the night;
　Come in the speaking silence of a dream;
Come with soft rounded cheeks and eyes as bright
　As sunlight on a stream;
　　Come back in tears,
O memory, hope, love of finished years.

O dream how sweet, too sweet, too bitter sweet,
　Whose wakening should have been in Paradise,
Where souls brimfull of love abide and meet;
　Where thirsting longing eyes
　　Watch the slow door
That opening, letting in, lets out no more.

Yet come to me in dreams, that I may live
　My very life again though cold in death:
Come back to me in dreams, that I may give
　Pulse for pulse, breath for breath:
　　Speak low, lean low,
As long ago, my love, how long ago.

She Walks in Beauty

GEORGE GORDON, LORD BYRON
(1788–1824)

She walks in beauty, like the night
   Of cloudless climes and starry skies;
And all that's best of dark and bright
   Meet in her aspect and her eyes:
Thus mellowed to that tender light
   Which heaven to gaudy day denies.

One shade the more, one ray the less,
   Had half impaired the nameless grace
Which waves in every raven tress,
   Or softly lightens o'er her face;
Where thoughts serenely sweet express
   How pure, how dear their dwelling place.

And on that cheek, and o'er that brow,
   So soft, so calm, yet eloquent,
The smiles that win, the tints that glow,
   But tell of days in goodness spent,
A mind at peace with all below,
   A heart whose love is innocent!

A Red, Red Rose

ROBERT BURNS
(1759–1796)

O, my luve is like a red, red rose,
 That's newly sprung in June.
O my luve is like the melodie,
 That's sweetly played in tune.

As fair art thou, my bonie lass,
 So deep in luve am I,
And I will luve thee still, my dear,
 Till a' the seas gang dry.

Till a' the seas gang dry, my dear,
 And the rocks melt wi' the sun!
And I will luve thee still, my dear,
 While the sands o' life shall run.

And fare thee weel, my only luve,
 And fare thee weel awhile!
And I will come again, my luve,
 Though it were ten thousand mile!

Now Sleeps the Crimson Petal

ALFRED, LORD TENNYSON

(1809–1892)

Now sleeps the crimson petal, now the white,
Nor waves the cypress in the palace walk:
Nor winks the gold fin in the porphyry font.
The firefly wakens. Waken thou with me.

Now droops the milk-white peacock like a ghost,
And like a ghost she glimmers on to me.

Now lies the Earth all Danaë to the stars,
And all thy heart lies open unto me.

Now slides the silent meteor on, and leaves
A shining furrow, as thy thoughts in me.

Now folds the lily all her sweetness up,
And slips into the bosom of the lake;
So fold thyself, my dearest, thou, and slip
Into my bosom and be lost in me.

Dover Beach
MATTHEW ARNOLD
(1822–1888)

The sea is calm to-night.
The tide is full, the moon lies fair
Upon the straits;—on the French coast the light
Gleams and is gone; the cliffs of England stand,
Glimmering and vast, out in the tranquil bay,
Come to the window, sweet is the night-air!
Only, from the long lien of spray
Where the sea meets the moon-blanched land,
Listen! you hear the grating roar
Of pebbles which the waves draw back, and fling.
At their return, up the high strand,
Begin, and cease, and then again begin,
With tremulous cadence slow, and bring
The eternal note of sadness in.

Sophocles long ago
Heard it on the Aegean and it brought
Into his mind the turbid ebb and flow
Of human misery; we
Find also in the sound a thought,
Hearing it by this distant northern sea.

The Sea of Faith
Was once, too, at the full, and round earth's shore
Lay like the folds of a bright girdle furled.
But now I only hear
Its melancholy, long, withdrawing roar,
Retreating, to the breath
Of the night-wind, down the vast edges drear
And naked shingles of the world.

Ah, love, let us be true
To one another! for the world, which seems
To lie before us like a land of dreams,
So various, so beautiful, so new,
Hath really neither joy, nor love, nor light,
Nor certitude, nor peace, nor help for pain;
And we are here as on a darkling plain
Swept with confused alarms of struggle and flight,
Where ignorant armies clash by night.

To Lucasta, on Going to the Wars

RICHARD LOVELACE
(1618–1658)

Tell me not, sweet, I am unkind,
    That from the nunnery
Of thy chaste breast and quiet mind
    To war and arms I fly.

True, a new mistress now I chase,
    The first foe in the field;
And with a stronger faith embrace
    A sword, a horse, a shield.

Yet this inconstancy is such
    As thou too shalt adore;
I could not love thee, dear, so much,
    Loved I not honor more.

My Life Closed Twice Before Its Close

EMILY DICKINSON

(1830–1886)

My life closed twice before its close—
It yet remains to see
If Immortality unveil
A third event to me

So huge, so hopeless to conceive
As these that twice befell.
Parting is all we know of heaven,
And all we need of hell.

Patterns

AMY LOWELL
(1874–1925)

I walk down the garden paths,
And all the daffodils
Are blowing, and the bright blue squills.
I walk down the patterned garden paths
In my stiff, brocaded gown.
With my powdered hair and jewelled fan,
I too am a rare
Pattern. As I wander down
The garden paths.

My dress is richly figured,
And the train
Makes a pink and silver stain
On the gravel, and the thrift
Of the borders,
Just a plate of current fashion
Tripping by in high-heeled, ribboned shoes.
Not a softness anywhere about me,
Only whalebone and brocade.
And I sink on a seat in the shade
Of a lime tree. For my passion
Wars against the stiff brocade.
The daffodils and squills
Flutter in the breeze
As they please.
And I weep;
For the lime tree is in blossom
And one small flower has dropped upon my bosom.

And the plashing of waterdrops
In the marble fountain
comes down the garden paths.
The dripping never stops.
Underneath my stiffened gown
Is the softness of a woman bathing in a marble basin,
A basin in the midst of hedges grown
So thick, she cannot see her lover hiding,
But she guesses he is near,
And the sliding of the water
Seems the stroking of a dear
Hand upon her.
What is Summer in a fine brocaded gown!
I should like to see it lying in a heap upon the
    ground.
All the pink and silver crumpled up on the ground.

I would be the pink and silver as I ran along the
    paths.
And he would stumble after,
Bewildered by my laughter.
I should see the sun flashing from his sword-hilt and
    buckles on his shoes.
I would choose
To lead him in a maze along the patterned paths.
A bright and laughing maze for my heavy-booted
    lover.
Till he caught me in the shade,
And the buttons of his waistcoat bruised my body as
    he clasped me,
Aching, melting, unafraid.
With the shadows of the leaves and the sundrops,
And the plopping of the waterdrops,
All about us in the open afternoon—
I am very like to swoon
With the weight of this brocade,
For the sun sifts through the shade.

Underneath the fallen blossom
In my bosom,
Is a letter I have hid.
It was brought to me this morning by a rider from
the Duke.
"Madam, we regret to inform you that Lord Hartwell
Died in action Thursday se'nnight."
As I read it in the white, morning sunlight,
The letters squirmed like snakes.
"Any answer, Madam," said my footman.
"No," I told him.
"See that the messenger takes some refreshment.
No, no answer."
And I walked into the garden,
Up and down the patterned paths,
In my stiff, correct brocade.
The blue and yellow flowers stood up proudly in the
sun,
Each one.
I stood upright too,
Held rigid to the pattern
By the stiffness of my gown,
Up and down I walked.
Up and down.

In a month he would have been my husband.
In a month, here, underneath this lime,
We would have broken the pattern;
He for me, and I for him,
He as Colonel, I as Lady,
On this shady seat.
He had a whim
That sunlight carried blessing.
And I answered, "It shall be as you have said."
Now he is dead.

In Summer and in Winter I shall walk
Up and down
The patterned garden paths
In my stiff, brocaded gown.
The squills and daffodils
Will give place to pillard roses, and to asters, and to
    snow.
I shall go
Up and down
In my gown.
Gorgeously arrayed,
Boned and stayed.
And the softness of my body will be guarded from
    embrace
By each button, hook, and lace.
For the man who should loose me is dead,
Fighting with the Duke in Flanders,
In a pattern called a war.
Christ! What are patterns for?

To—
Percy Bysshe Shelley
(1792–1822)

Music, when soft voices die,
Vibrates in the memory—
Odors, when sweet violets sicken,
Live within the sense they quicken.

Rose leaves, when the rose is dead,
Are heaped for the belovèd's bed;
And so thy thoughts, when thou art gone,
Love itself shall slumber on.

She Dwelt Among the Untrodden Ways

WILLIAM WORDSWORTH
(1770–1850)

She dwelt among the untrodden ways
   Beside the springs of Dove,
A Maid whom there were none to praise
   And very few to love:

A violet by a mossy stone
   Half hidden from the eye!
—Fair as a star, when only one
   Is shining in the sky.

She lived unknown, and few could know
   When Lucy ceased to be;
But she is in her grave, and, oh,
   The difference to me!

Annabel Lee

EDGAR ALLAN POE
(1809–1849)

It was many and many a year ago,
   In a kingdom by the sea
That a maiden there lived whom you may know
   By the name of Annabel Lee;—
And this maiden she lived with no other thought
   Than to love and be loved by me.

I was a child and *she* was a child,
   In this kingdom by the sea,
But we loved with a love that was more than love—
   I and my Annabel Lee—
With a love that the wingèd seraphs in Heaven
   Coveted her and me.

And this was the reason that, long ago,
   In this kingdom by the sea,
A wind blew out of a cloud, chilling
   My beautiful Annabel Lee;
So that her high-born kinsmen came
   And bore her away from me,
To shut her up in a sepulcher
   In this kingdom by the sea.

The angels, not half so happy in Heaven,
   Went envying her and me:—
Yes!—that was the reason (as all men know,
   In this kingdom by the sea)
That the wind came out of the cloud, by night,
   Chilling and killing my Annabel Lee.

But our love it was stronger by far than the love
   Of those who were older than we—
   Of many far wiser than we—
And neither the angels in Heaven above,
   Nor the demons down under the sea,
Can ever dissever my soul from the soul
   Of the beautiful Annabel Lee:—

For the moon never beams without bringing me
     dreams
   Of the beautiful Annabel Lee;
And the stars never rise but I feel the bright eyes
   Of the beautiful Annabel Lee;
And so, all the night-tide, I lie down by the side
Of my darling,—my darling,—my life and my bride,
   In the sepulcher there by the sea—
In her tomb by the sounding sea.

Summum Bonum

ROBERT BROWNING

(1812-1889)

All the breath and the bloom of the
   year in the bag of one bee:
All the wonder and wealth of the mine in
   the heart of one gem:
In the core of one pearl all the shade and the
   shine of the sea:
Breath and bloom, shade and shine,—wonder,
   wealth, and—how far above them—
     Truth, that's brighter than gem,
     Trust, that's purer than pearl,—
Brightest truth, purest trust in the universe—
   all were for me
     In the kiss of one girl.

To Althea, from Prison

RICHARD LOVELACE
(1618–1658)

When Love with unconfinèd wings
   Hovers within my gates,
And my divine Althea brings
   To whisper at the grates;
When I lie tangled in her hair
   And fettered to her eye,
The birds that wanton in the air
   Know no such liberty.

When flowing cups run swiftly round
   With no allaying Thames,
Our careless heads with roses bound,
   Our hearts with loyal flames;
When thirsty grief in wine we steep,
   When healths and draughts go free,
Fishes that tipple in the deep
   Know no such liberty.

When, like committed linnets, I
   With shriller throat shall sing
The sweetness, mercy, majesty,
   And glories of my king;
When I shall voice aloud how good
   He is, how great should be,
Enlargèd winds, that curl the flood,
   Know no such liberty.

Stone walls do not a prison make,
 Nor iron bars a cage;
Minds innocent and quiet take
 That for an hermitage;
If I have freedom in my love,
 And in my soul am free,
Angels alone, that soar above,
 Enjoy such liberty.

To Helen

EDGAR ALLAN POE
(1809–1849)

Helen, thy beauty is to me
 Like those Nicaean barks of yore,
That gently, o'er a perfumed sea,
 The weary, wayworn wanderer bore
 To his own native shore.

On desperate seas long wont to roam,
 Thy hyacinth hair, thy classic face,
Thy Naiad airs have brought me home
 To the glory that was Greece
 And the grandeur that was Rome.

Lo! in yon brilliant window-niche
 How statue-like I see thee stand,
The agate lamp within thy hand!
 Ah, Psyche, from the regions which
 Are Holy Land!

The Indian Serenade

PERCY BYSSHE SHELLEY
(1792–1822)

I arise from dreams of thee
In the first sweet sleep of night,
When the winds are breathing low,
And the stars are shining bright:
I arise from dreams of thee,
And a spirit in my feet
Hath led me—who knows how?
To thy chamber window, Sweet!

The wandering airs they faint
On the dark, the silent stream—
The Champak odors fail
Like sweet thoughts in a dream;
The nightingale's complaint,
It dies upon her heart;—
As I must on thine,
Oh, belovèd as thou art!

Oh lift me from the grass!
I die! I faint! I fail!
Let thy love in kisses rain
On my lips and eyelids pale.
My cheek is cold and white, alas!
My heart beats loud and fast;—
Oh! press it to thine own again,
Where it will break at last.

When You Are Old

WILLIAM BUTLER YEATS
(1865–1939)

When you are old and gray and full of sleep,
And nodding by the fire, take down this book,
And slowly read, and dream of the soft look
Your eyes had once, and of their shadows deep;

How many loved your moments of glad grace,
And loved your beauty with love false or true;
But one man loved the pilgrim soul in you,
And loved the sorrows of your changing face.

And bending down beside the glowing bars
Murmur, a little sadly, how love fled
And paced upon the mountains overhead
And hid his face amid a crowd of stars.

A Drinking Song

WILLIAM BUTLER YEATS
(1865–1939)

Wine comes in at the mouth
And love comes in at the eye;
That's all we shall know for truth
Before we grow old and die.
I lift the glass to my mouth,
I look at you, and I sigh.

somewhere i have never travelled

e. e. cummings

(1894-1962)

somewhere i have never travelled,gladly beyond
any experience,your eyes have their silence:
in your most frail gesture are things which enclose me,
or which i cannot touch because they are too near

your slightest look easily will unclose me
though i have closed myself as fingers,
you open always petal by petal myself as Spring opens
(touching skilfully,mysteriously) her first rose

or if your wish be to close me,i and
my life will shut very beautifully,suddenly,
as when the heart of this flower imagines
the snow carefully everywhere descending;

nothing which we are to perceive in this world equals
the power of your intense fragility:whose texture
compels me with the color of its countries,
rendering death and forever with each breathing

(i do not know what it is about you that closes
and opens;only something in me understands
the voice of your eyes is deeper than all roses)
nobody,not even the rain,has such small hands

Marriage Morning

Alfred, Lord Tennyson
(1809–1892)

Light, so low upon earth,
    You send a flash to the sun.
Here is the golden close of love,
    All my wooing is done.
Oh, the woods and the meadows,
    Woods where we hid from the wet,
Stiles where we stay'd to be kind,
    Meadows in which we met!

Light, so low in the vale
    You flash and lighten afar,
For this is the golden morning of love,
    And you are his morning star.
Flash, I am coming, I come,
    By meadow and stile and wood,
Oh, lighten into my eyes and heart,
    Into my heart and my blood!

Heart, are you great enough
    For a love that never tires?
O heart, are you great enough for love?
    I have heard of thorns and briers.
Over the thorns and briers,
    Over the meadows and stiles,
Over the world to the end of it
    Flash for a million miles.

Let Me Not to the Marriage of True Minds

WILLIAM SHAKESPEARE

(1564–1616)

Let me not to the marriage of true minds
Admit impediments. Love is not love
Which alters when it alteration finds,
Or bends with the remover to remove:
O, no! it is an ever-fixèd mark
That looks on tempests and is never shaken;
It is the star to every wandering bark,
Whose worth's unknown, although his height be
    taken.
Love's not Time's fool, though rosy lips and cheeks
Within his bending sickle's compass come;
Love alters not with his brief hours and weeks,
But bears it out even to the edge of doom.
If this be error and upon me proved,
I never writ, nor no man ever loved.

Believe Me, If All Those Endearing Young Charms

Thomas Moore
(1779–1852)

Believe me, if all those endearing young charms,
   Which I gaze on so fondly to-day,
Were to change by to-morrow, and fleet in my arms,
   Like fairy-gifts fading away,
Thou wouldst still be adored, as this moment thou
     art,
   Let thy loveliness fade as it will,
And around the dear ruin each wish of my heart
   Would entwine itself verdantly still.

It is not while beauty and youth are thine own,
   And thy cheeks unprofaned by a tear,
That the fervor and faith of a soul may be known,
   To which time will but make thee more dear!
No, the heart that has truly loved never forgets,
   But as truly loves on to the close,
As the sunflower turns to her god when he sets
   The same look which she turned when he rose!

The Country of Marriage

WENDELL BERRY
(b. 1934)

1

I dream of you walking at night along the streams
of the country of my birth, warm blooms and the
    nightsongs
of birds opening around you as you walk.
You are holding in your body the dark seed of my
    sleep.

2

This comes after silence. Was it something I said
that bound me to you, some mere promise
or, worse, the fear of loneliness and death?
A man lost in the woods in the dark, I stood
still and said nothing. And then there rose in me,
like the earth's empowering brew rising
in root and branch, the words of a dream of you
I did not know I had dreamed. I was a wanderer
who feels the solace of his native land
under his feet again and moving in his blood.
I went on, blind and faithful. Where I stepped
my track was there to steady me. It was no abyss
that lay before me, but only the level ground.

3
Sometimes our life reminds me
of a forest in which there is a graceful clearing
and in that opening a house,
an orchard and garden,
comfortable shades, and flowers
red and yellow in the sun, a pattern
made in the light for the light to return to.
The forest is mostly dark, its ways
to be made anew day after day, the dark
richer than the light and more blessed
provided we stay brave
enough to keep on going in.

4
How many times have I come into you out of my
    head
with joy, if ever a man was,
for to approach you I have given up the light
and all directions. I come to you
lost, wholly trusting, as a man who goes
into the forest unarmed. It is as though I descend
slowly earthward out of the air. I rest in peace
in you, when I arrive at last.

True Love

JUDITH VIORST

(b. 1931)

It is true love because

I put on eyeliner and a concerto and make pungent
   observations about the great issues of the day

Even when there's no one here but him,

And because

I do not resent watching the Green Bay Packers

Even though I am philosophically opposed to
   football,

And because

When he is late for dinner and I know he must be
   either having an affair or lying dead in the
   middle of the street,

I always hope he's dead.

It's true love because

If he said quit drinking martinis but I kept drinking
   them and the next morning I couldn't get out of
   bed,

He wouldn't tell me he told me,

And because

He is willing to wear unironed undershorts

Out of respect for the fact that I am philosophically
   opposed to ironing,

And because

If his mother was drowning and I was drowning and
   he had to choose one of us to save,

He says he'd save me.

It's true love because

When he went to San Francisco on business while I
   had to stay home with the painters and the
   exterminator and the baby who was getting the
   chicken pox,

He understood why I hated him,

And because

When I said that playing the stock market was
   juvenile and irresponsible and then the stock I
   wouldn't let him buy went up twenty-six points,

I understood why he hated me,

And because

Despite cigarette cough, tooth decay, acid
   indigestion, dandruff, and other features of
   married life that tend to dampen the fires of
   passion,

We still feel something

We can call

True love.

Love 20¢ the First Quarter Mile

(1902-1961)

All right. I may have lied to you and about you, and
    made a few pronouncements a bit too sweeping,
    perhaps, and possibly forgotten to tag the bases
    here or there,
And damned your extravagance, and maligned your
    tastes, and libeled your relatives, and slandered a
    few of your friends,
O.K.,
   Nevertheless, come back.

Come home. I will agree to forget the statements that
    you issued so copiously to the neighbors and the
    press,
And you will forget that figment of your
    imagination, the blonde from Detroit;
I will agree that your lady friend who lives above us
    is not crazy, bats, nutty as they come, but on the
    contrary rather bright,
And you will concede that poor old Steinberg is
    neither a drunk, nor a swindler, but simply a
    guy, on the eccentric side, trying to get along.
(Are you listening, you bitch, and have you got this
    straight?)

Because I forgive you, yes, for everything.
I forgive you for being beautiful and generous and
    wise,

I forgive you, to put it simply, for being alive, and
    pardon you, in short, for being you.

Because tonight you are in my hair and eyes,
And every street light that our taxi passes shows me
    you again, still you,
And because tonight all other nights are black, all
    other hours are cold and far away, and now, this
    minute, the stars are very near and bright

Come back. We will have a celebration to end all
    celebrations.
We will invite the undertaker who lives beneath us,
    and a couple of boys from the office, and some
    other friends.
And Steinberg, who is off the wagon, and that insane
    woman who lives upstairs, and a few reporters, if
    anything should break.

A Woman's Last Word

Robert Browning

(1812-1889)

Let's contend no more, Love,
　　Strive nor weep:
All be as before, Love,
　　—Only sleep!

What so wild as words are?
　　I and thou
In debate, as birds are,
　　Hawk on bough!

See the creature stalking
　　While we speak!
Hush and hide the talking,
　　Cheek on cheek!

What so false as truth is,
　　False to thee?
Where the serpent's tooth is,
　　Shun the tree—

Where the apple reddens
　　Never pry—
Lest we lose our Edens,
　　Eve and I.

Be a god and hold me
　　With a charm!
Be a man and fold me
　　With thine arm!

Teach me, only teach, Love!
   As I ought.
I will speak thy speech, Love,
   Think thy thought—

Meet, if thou require it,
   Both demands,
Laying flesh and spirit
   In thy hands.

That shall be tomorrow,
   Not tonight:
I must bury sorrow
   Out of sight:

—Must a little weep, Love,
   (Foolish me!)
And so fall asleep, Love,
   Loved by thee.

Song to Celia

BEN JONSON
(1573–1637)

Drink to me only with thine eyes,
  And I will pledge with mine;
Or leave a kiss but in the cup,
  And I'll not look for wine.
The thirst that from the soul doth rise
  Doth ask a drink divine;
But might I of Jove's nectar sup,
  I would not change for thine.

I sent thee late a rosy wreath,
  Not so much honoring thee
As giving it a hope that there
  It could not withered be.
But thou thereon didst only breathe,
  And sent'st it back to me;
Since when it grows, and smells, I swear,
  Not of itself but thee.

Lady Greensleeves

UNKNOWN
(circa 1580)

Alas, my love, ye do me wrong,
   To cast me off disc'urteously:
And I have loved you so long,
   Delighting in your company.

Greensleeves was all my joy,
   Greensleeves was my delight:
Greensleeves was my heart of gold,
   And who but Lady Greensleeves.

I have been ready at your hand,
   To grant what ever you would crave.
I have both waged life and land,
   Your love and good will for to have.

   Greensleeves was all my joy, etc.

I bought thee kerchers to thy head,
   That were wrought fine and gallantly:
I kept thee both at board and bed,
   Which cost my purse well favouredly,

Greensleeves was all my joy, etc.

I bought thee petticoats of the best,
   The cloth so fine as fine might be:
I gave thee jewels for thy chest,
   And all this cost I spent on thee.

Thy smock of silk, both fair and white,
   With gold embroidered gorgeously:
Thy petticoat of sendal right:
   And thus I bought thee gladly.

Thy girdle of gold so red,
  With pearls bedecked sumptuously:
The like no other lasses had,
  And yet thou wouldst not love me,

Thy purse and eke thy gay guilt knives,
  Thy pincase gallant to the eye:
No better wore the burgess wives,
  And yet thou wouldst not love me.

Thy crimson stockings all of silk,
  With gold all wrought above the knee,
Thy pumps as white as was the milk,
  And yet thou wouldst not love me.

Thy gown was of the grossy green,
  Thy sleeves of satin hanging by:
Which made thee be our harvest Queen,
  And yet thou wouldst not love me.

Thy garters fringed with the gold,
  And silver aglets hanging by,
Which made thee blithe for to behold,
  And yet thou wouldst not love me.

My gayest gelding I thee gave,
  To ride where ever liked thee,
No Lady ever was so brave,
  And yet thou wouldst not love me.

My men were clothed all in green,
  And they did ever wait on thee:
All this was gallant to be seen,
  And yet thou wouldst not love me.

They set thee up, they took thee down,
    They served thee with humility,
Thy foot might not once touch the ground,
    And yet thou wouldst not love me.

For every morning when thou rose,
    I sent thee dainties orderly:
To cheer thy stomach from all woes,
    And yet thou wouldst not love me.

Thou couldst desire no earthly thing.
    But still thou hadst it readily:
Thy music still to play and sing,
    And yet thou wouldst not love me.

And who did pay for all this gear,
    That thou didst spend when pleased thee?
Even I that am rejected here,
    And thou disdainst to love me.

Well, I will pray to God on high,
    That thou my constancy mayst see:
And that yet once before I die,
    Thou wilt vouchsafe to love me.

Greensleeves now farewell, adieu,
    God I pray to prosper thee:
For I am still thy lover true,
    Come once again and love me.

I Think I Should Have Loved You Presently

EDNA ST. VINCENT MILLAY

(1892–1950)

I think I should have loved you presently,
And given in earnest words I flung in jest;
And lifted honest eyes for you to see,
And caught your hand against my cheek and breast;
And all my pretty follies flung aside
That won you to me, and beneath your gaze,
Naked of reticence and shorn of pride,
Spread like a chart my little wicked ways.
I, that had been to you, had you remained,
But one more waking from a recurrent dream,
Cherish no less the certain stakes I gained,
And walk your memory's halls, austere, supreme,
A ghost in marble of a girl you knew
Who would have loved you in a day or two.

The Taxi

AMY LOWELL
(1874–1925)

When I go away from you
The world beats dead
Like a slackened drum.
I call out for you against the jutted stars
And shout into the ridges of the wind.
Streets coming fast,
One after the other,
Wedge you away from me,
And the lamps of the city prick my eyes
So that I can no longer see your face.
Why should I leave you,
To wound myself upon the sharp edges of the night?

Love Recognized

ROBERT PENN WARREN

(b. 1905)

There are many things in the world and you
Are one of them. Many things keep happening and
You are one of them, and the happening that
Is you keeps falling like snow
On the landscape of not-you, hiding hideousness,
    until
The streets and the world of wrath are choked with
    snow.

How many things have become silent? Traffic
Is throttled. The mayor
Has been, clearly, remiss, and the city
Was totally unprepared for such a crisis. Nor
Was I—yes, why should this happen to me?
I have always been a law-abiding citizen.

But you, like snow, like love, keep falling,

And it is not certain that the world will not be
Covered in a glitter of crystalline whiteness.

Silence.

The Face of Helen

From *Dr. Faustus*

CHRISTOPHER MARLOWE

(1564–1593)

Was this the face that launched a thousand ships,
And burnt the topless towers of Ilium?
Sweet Helen, make me immortal with a kiss.

(Kisses her.)

Her lips suck forth my soul: see, where it flies!
Come, Helen, come, give me my soul again.
Here will I dwell, for heaven is in these lips,
And all is dross that is not Helena.
I will be Paris, and for love of thee,
Instead of Troy, shall Wertenberg be sacked;
And I will combat with weak Menelaus,
And wear thy colors on my plumed crest;
Yes, I will wound Achilles in the heel,
And then return to Helen for a kiss.
O, thou are fairer than the evening air
Clad in the beauty of a thousand stars;
Brighter art thou than flaming Jupiter
When he appeared to hapless Semele;
More lovely than the monarch of the sky
In wanton Arethusa's azured arms;
And none but thou shalt be my paramour.

La Belle Dame sans Merci

JOHN KEATS
(1795–1821)

O what can ail thee, knight-at-arms,
    Alone and palely loitering?
The sedge has withered from the lake,
    And no birds sing.

O what can ail thee, knight-at-arms,
    So haggard and so woe-begone?
The squirrel's granary is full,
    And the harvest's done.

I see a lily on thy brow
    With anguish moist and fever dew,
And on thy cheek a fading rose
    Fast withereth too.

I met a lady in the meads,
    Full beautiful—a faery's child;
Her hair was long, her foot was light,
    And her eyes were wild.

I made a garland for her head,
    And bracelets too, and fragrant zone;
She looked at me as she did love,
    And made sweet moan.

I set her on my pacing steed,
    And nothing else saw all day long,
For sidelong would she bend, and sing
    A faery's song.

She found me roots of relish sweet,
  And honey wild, and manna dew,
And sure in language strange she said—
  "I love thee true!"

She took me to her elfin grot,
  And there she wept and sighed full sore,
And there I shut her wild wild eyes
  With kisses four.

And there she lullèd me asleep,
  And there I dreamed—ah! woe betide!
The latest dream I ever dreamed
  On the cold hill's side.

I saw pale kings and princes too,
  Pale warriors, death-pale were they all;
They cried—"La Belle Dame sans Merci
  Thee hath in thrall!"

I saw their starved lips in the gloam,
  With horrid warning gapèd wide,
And I awoke and found me here,
  On the cold hill's side.

And this is why I sojourn here,
  Alone and palely loitering,
Though the sedge is withered from the lake
  And no birds sing.

The Mirabeau Bridge

GUILLAUME APOLLINAIRE
(1880–1918)

Under the Mirabeau Bridge the Seine
Flows and our love
Must I be reminded again
How joy came always after pain

Night comes the hour is rung
The days go I remain

Hands within hands we stand face to face
While underneath
The bridge of our arms passes
The loose wave of our gazing which is endless

Night comes the hour is rung
The days go I remain

Love slips away like this water flowing
Love slips away
How slow life is in its going
And hope is so violent a thing

Night comes the hour is rung
The days go I remain

The days pass the weeks pass and are gone
Neither time that is gone
Nor love ever returns again
Under the Mirabeau Bridge flows the Seine

Night comes the hour is rung
The days go I remain

Translated by W. S. Merwin

With How Sad Steps, O Moon

SIR PHILIP SIDNEY

(1554–1586)

With how sad steps, O Moon, thou climb'st the
    skies!
How silently, and with how wan a face!
What, may it be that even in heavenly place
That busy archer his sharp arrows tries?
Sure, if that long-with-love-acquainted eyes
Can judge of love, thou feel'st a lover's case,
I read it in thy looks; thy languished grace,
To me, that feel the like, thy state descries.
Then, even of fellowship, O Moon, tell me,
Is constant love deemed there but want of wit?
Are beauties there as proud as here they be?
Do they above love to be loved, and yet
Those lovers scorn whom that love doth possess?
Do they call virtue there ungratefulness?

Remembrance
SIR THOMAS WYATT
(1503–1542)

They flee from me, that sometime did me seek
  With naked foot, stalking in my chamber.
I have seen them gentle, tame, and meek,
  That now are wild, and do not remember
  That sometime they put themselves in danger
    To take bread at my hand; and now they range
    Busily seeking with a continual change.

Thanked be fortune it hath been otherwise
  Twenty times better; but once, in special,
In thin array, after a pleasant guise,
  When her loose gown from her shoulders did fall,
  And she me caught in her arms long and small,
    Therewith all sweetly did me kiss
    And softly said, 'Dear heart how like you this?'

It was no dream; I lay broad waking:
  But all is turned, through my gentleness,
Into a strange fashion of forsaking;
  And I have leave to go of her goodness,
  And she also to use newfangleness.
    But since that I so kindly am served,
    I would fain know what she hath deserved.

The Night Has a Thousand Eyes

FRANCIS WILLIAM BOURDILLON
(1852–1921)

The night has a thousand eyes,
    And the day but one;
Yet the light of the bright world dies
    With the dying sun.

The mind has a thousand eyes,
    And the heart but one;
Yet the light of a whole life dies
    When love is done.

Jenny Kiss'd Me

JAMES HENRY LEIGH HUNT
(1784–1859)

Jenny kissed me when we met,
Jumping from the chair she sat in.
Time, you thief! who love to get
Sweets into your list, put that in.
Say I'm weary, say I'm sad;
Say that health and wealth have missed me;
Say I'm growing old, but add—
Jenny kissed me.

An Old Sweetheart of Mine

JAMES WHITCOMB RILEY

(1849–1916)

An old sweetheart of mine!—Is this her presence here with me,
Or but a vain creation of a lover's memory?
A fair, illusive vision that would vanish into air,
Dared I even touch the silence with the whisper of a prayer?

Nay, let me then believe in all the blended false and true—
The semblance of the old love and the substance of the *new*,—
The *then* of changeless sunny days—the *now* of shower and shine—
But Love forever smiling—as that old sweetheart of mine.

This ever restful sense of *home* though shouts ring in the hall,—
The easy chair—the old book-shelves and prints along the wall;
The rare *Habanas* in their box, or gaunt churchwarden-stem
That often wags, above the jar, derisively at them.

As one who cons at evening o'er an album, all alone,
And muses on the faces of the friends that he has known,
So I turn the leaves of Fancy, till, in a shadowy design,
I find the smiling features of an old sweetheart of mine.

The lamplight seems to glimmer with a flicker of
     surprise,
As I turn it low—to rest me of the dazzle in my eyes,
And light my pipe in silence, save a sigh that seems
     to yoke
Its fate with my tobacco and to vanish with the
     smoke.

'Tis a *fragrant* retrospection,—for the loving
     thoughts that start
Into being are like perfume from the blossom of the
     heart;
And to dream the old dreams over is a luxury
     divine—
When my truant fancies wander with that old
     sweetheart of mine.

Though I hear beneath my study, like a fluttering of
     wings,
The voices of my children and the mother as she
     sings—
I feel no twinge of conscience to deny me any theme
When Care has cast her anchor in the harbor of a
     dream—

In fact, to speak in earnest, I believe it adds a charm
To spice the good a trifle with a little dust of
     harm,—
For I find an extra flavor in Memory's mellow wine
That makes me drink the deeper to that old
     sweetheart of mine.

O Childhood-days enchanted! O the magic of the
     Spring!—
With all green boughs to blossom white, and all
     bluebirds to sing!
When all the air, to toss and quaff, made life a
     jubilee
And changed the children's song and laugh to
     shrieks of ecstasy.

With eyes half closed in clouds that ooze from lips
     that taste, as well,
The peppermint and cinnamon, I hear the old school
     bell,
And from "Recess" romp in again from "Blackman's"
     broken line,
To smile, behind my "lesson", at that old sweetheart
     of mine.

A face of lily beauty, with a form of airy grace,
Float out of my tobacco as the Genii from the vase;
And I thrill beneath the glances of a pair of azure
     eyes
As glowing as the summer and as tender as the skies.

I can see the pink sunbonnet and the little checkered
     dress
She wore when first I kissed her and she answered
     the caress
With the written declaration that, "as surely as the
     vine
Grew 'round the stump" she loved me—that old
     sweetheart of mine.

Again I made her presents, in a really helpless way,—
The big "Rhode Island Greening"—I was hungry,
    too, that day!—
But I follow her from Spelling, with her hand behind
    her—so—
And I slip the apple in it—and the Teacher doesn't
    know!

I give my *treasures* to her—all,—my pencil—blue and
    red;—
And, if little girls played marbles, *mine* should all be
    hers, instead!
But *she* gave me her *photograph*, and printed "Ever
    Thine"
Across the back—in blue and red—that old
    sweetheart of mine!

And again I feel the pressure of her slender little
    hand,
As we used to talk together of the future we had
    planned,—
When I should be a poet, and with nothing else to
    do
But write the tender verses that she set the music
    to . . .

Then we should live together in a cozy little cot
Hid in a nest of roses, with a fairy garden spot,
Where the vines were ever fruited, and the weather
    ever fine,
And the birds were ever singing for that old
    sweetheart of mine.

When I should be her lover forever and a day,
And she my faithful sweetheart till the golden hair
    was gray;
And we should be so happy that when either's lips
    were dumb
They would not smile in Heaven till the other's kiss
    had come.

But, ah! my dream is broken by a step upon the stair,
And the door is softly opened, and—my wife is
    standing there;
Yet with eagerness and rapture all my vision I
    resign,—
To greet the *living* presence of that old sweetheart of
    mine.

She Was a Phantom of Delight

WILLIAM WORDSWORTH
(1770–1850)

She was a phantom of delight
When first she gleamed upon my sight;
A lovely apparition, sent
To be a moment's ornament;
Her eyes as stars of twilight fair;
Like twilight's, too, her dusky hair;
But all things else about her drawn
From May-time and the cheerful dawn;
A dancing shape, an image gay,
To haunt, to startle, and waylay.

I saw her upon nearer view,
A spirit, yet a woman too!
Her household motions light and free,
And step of virgin liberty;
A countenance in which did meet
Sweet records, promises as sweet;
A creature not too bright or good
For human nature's daily food,
For transient sorrows, simple wiles,
Praise, blame, love, kisses, tears, and smiles.

And now I see with eye serene
The very pulse of the machine;
A being breathing thoughtful breath,
A traveler between life and death;
The reason firm, the temperate will,
Endurance, foresight, strength, and skill;
A perfect woman, nobly planned
To warn, to comfort, and command;
And yet a spirit still, and bright
With something of angelic light.

Recuerdo

EDNA ST. VINCENT MILLAY

(1892–1950)

We were very tired, we were very merry—
We had gone back and forth all night on the ferry.
It was bare and bright, and smelled like a stable—
But we looked into a fire, we leaned across a table,
We lay on a hill-top underneath the moon;
And the whistles kept blowing, and the dawn came
soon.

We were very tired, we were very merry—
We had gone back and forth all night on the ferry;
And you ate an apple, and I ate a pear,
From a dozen of each we had bought somewhere;
And the sky went wan, and the wind came cold,
And the sun rose dripping, a bucketful of gold.

We were very tired, we were very merry,
We had gone back and forth all night on the ferry.
We hailed, "Good-morrow, mother!" to a shawl-
covered head,
And bought a morning paper, which neither of us
read;
And she wept, "God bless you!" for the apples and
pears,
And we gave her all our money but our subway fares.

A Birthday

CHRISTINA ROSSETTI
(1830–1894)

My heart is like a singing bird
  Whose nest is in a watered shoot;
My heart is like an apple-tree
  Whose boughs are bent with thick-set fruit;
My heart is like a rainbow shell
  That paddles in a halcyon sea;
My heart is gladder than all these,
  Because my love is come to me.

Raise me a dais of silk and down;
  Hang it with vair and purple dyes;
Carve it in doves and pomegranates,
  And peacocks with a hundred eyes;
Work it in gold and silver grapes,
  In leaves and silver fleur-de-lys;
Because the birthday of my life
  Is come, my love is come to me.

Wild Nights

EMILY DICKINSON
(1830–1886)

Wild nights! Wild nights!
Were I with thee,
Wild nights should be
Our luxury!

Futile the winds
To a heart in port—
Done with the compass,
Done with the chart.

Rowing in Eden!
Ah! the sea!
Might I but moor
Tonight in thee!

I Have Come to You to Greet You

AFANASY FET (SHENSHIN)
(1820–1892)

I have come to you to greet you,
To tell you that the sun is up:
The sun's hot light now waits to greet you
And trembles through the leaves and sap;

To tell you that the forest is awake,
Ferociously awake, every branch is budding,
Each bird awake
And full of spring:

To tell you that I come again
(I do not know what I shall sing)
With yesterday's same passion
To serve you—a happy song is ripening.

Translated by James Greene

One Day I Wrote Her Name Upon the Strand

EDMUND SPENSER
(1552-1599)

One day I wrote her name upon the strand,
But came the waves and washed it away:
Agayne I wrote it with a second hand,
But came the tyde, and made my paynes his pray.
Vayne man, sayd she, that doest in vaine assay,
A mortall thing so to immortalize,
For I my selve shall lyke to this decay,
And eek my name bee wyped out lykewize.
Not so, (quod I) let baser things devize
To dy in dust, but you shall live by fame:
My verse your vertues rare shall eternize,
And in the hevens wryte your glorious name.
Where whenas death shall al the world subdew,
Our love shall live, and later life renew.

Love Is Enough

WILLIAM MORRIS
(1834–1896)

Love is enough: though the World be a-waning,
And the woods have no voice but the voice of
    complaining,
  Though the skies be too dark for dim eyes to
    discover
The gold-cups and daisies fair blooming thereunder,
Though the hills be held shadows, and the sea a dark
    wonder,
  And this day draw a veil over all deeds pass'd over,
Yet their hands shall not tremble, their feet shall not
    falter:
The void shall not weary, the fear shall not alter
  These lips and these eyes of the loved and the lover.

What Lips My Lips Have Kissed

EDNA ST. VINCENT MILLAY
(1892–1950)

What lips my lips have kissed, and where, and why,
I have forgotten, and what arms have lain
Under my head till morning; but the rain
Is full of ghosts tonight, that tap and sigh
Upon the glass and listen for reply,
And in my heart there stirs a quiet pain
For unremembered lads that not again
Will turn to me at midnight with a cry.
Thus in the winter stands the lonely tree,
Nor knows what birds have vanished one by one,
Yet knows its boughs more silent than before:
I cannot say what loves have come and gone,
I only know that summer sang in me
A little while, that in me sings no more.

How Like a Winter Hath My Absence Been

WILLIAM SHAKESPEARE

(1564–1616)

How like a winter hath my absence been
From thee, the pleasure of the fleeting year!
What freezings have I felt, what dark days seen!
What old December's bareness everywhere!
And yet this time removed was summer's time,
The teeming autumn, big with rich increase,
Bearing the wanton burden of the prime,
Like widowed wombs after their lords' decease:
Yet this abundant issue seemed to me
But hope of orphans and unfathered fruit;
For summer and his pleasures wait on thee,
And, thou away, the very birds are mute;
Or, if they sing, 'tis with so dull a cheer
That leaves look pale, dreading the winter's near.

Bonny Barbara Allan

UNKNOWN
(sixteenth or seventeenth century)

There are many versions of this sad ballad of a powerful, stubborn, and ill-fated love. Brought by settlers from England to America, it became a favorite in the new land.

It was in and about the Martinmas time,
    When the green leaves were a falling,
That Sir John Graeme, in the West Country,
    Fell in love with Barbara Allan.

He sent his man down through the town,
    To the place where she was dwelling:
"O haste and come to my master dear,
    Gin ye be Barbara Allan."

O hooly, hooly rose she up,
    To the place where he was lying,
And when she drew the curtain by,
    "Young man, I think you're dying."

"O it's I'm sick, and very, very sick,
And 'tis a' for Barbara Allan:"
"O the better for me ye's never be,
    Tho your heart's blood were a spilling.

"O dinna ye mind, young man," said she,
    "When ye was in the tavern a drinking,
That ye made the healths gae round and round,
    And slighted Barbara Allan?"

He turnd his face unto the wall,
   And death was with him dealing:
"Adieu, adieu, my dear friends all,
   And be kind to Barbara Allan."

And slowly, slowly raise she up,
   And slowly, slowly left him,
And sighing said, she could not stay,
   Since death of life had reft him.

She had not gane a mile but twa,
   When she heard the dead-bell ringing,
And every jow that the dead-bell geid,
   It cry'd, Woe to Barbara Allan!

"O mother, mother, make my bed!
   O make it saft and narrow!
Since my love died for me to-day,
   I'll die for him to-morrow."

Love Will Find Out the Way

UNKNOWN
(circa 1632)

Over the mountains
  And under the waves,
Over the fountains
  And under the graves,
Over floods which are the deepest
  Which do Neptune obey,
Over rocks which are steepest,
  Love will find out the way.

Where there is no place
  For the glow-worm to lie;
Where there is no space
  For receipt of a fly;
Where the gnat she dares not venter,
  Lest herself fast she lay;
But if Love come, he will enter,
  And will find out the way.

You may esteem him
  A child by his force,
Or you may deem him
  A coward, which is worse;
But if he whom Love doth honour
  Be concealed from the day,
Set a thousand guards upon him,
  Love will find out the way.

Some think to lose him,
   Which is too unkind;
And some do suppose him,
   Poor heart, to be blind;
If that he were hidden,
   Do the best that you may,
Blind Love, if so you call him,
   Will find out the way.

Well may the eagle
   Stoop down to the fist;
Or you may inveigle
   The phoenix of the east;
With fear the tiger's moved
   To give over his prey,
But never stop a lover,
   He will post on his way.

From Dover to Berwick,
   And nations throughout,
Brave Guy of Warwick,
   That champion so stout,
With his warlike behaviour,
   Through the world he did stray
To win his Phyllis' favour—
   Love will find out the way.

In order next enters
   Bevis so brave;
After adventures,
   And policy grave,
To see whom he desired,
   His Josian so gay,
For whom his heart was fired,
   Love found out the way.

The Gordian knot
    Which true lovers knit,
Undo you cannot,
    Nor yet break it;
Make use of your inventions
    Their fancies to betray,
To frustrate your intentions
    Love will find out the way.

From court to the cottage,
    In bower and in hall,
From the king unto the beggar,
    Love conquers all;
Though ne'er so stout and lordly,
    Strive, do what you may,
Yet, be you ne'er so hardy,
    Love will find out the way.

Love hath power over princes
    And greatest emperor;
In any provinces,
    Such is Love's power,
There is no resisting,
    But him to obey;
In spite of all contesting,
    Love will find out the way.

If that he were hidden,
    And all men that are,
Were strictly forbidden
    That place to declare,
Winds that have no abidings,
    Pitying their delay,
Will come and bring him tidings,
    And direct him the way.

If the earth should part him
    He would gallop it o'er;
If the seas should o'erthwart him,
    He would swim to the shore;
Should his love become a swallow,
    Through the air to stray,
Love would lend wings to follow,
    And will find out the way.

There is no striving
    To cross his intent,
There is no contriving
    His plots to prevent;
But if once the message greet him
    That his true love doth stay,
If death should come and meet him,
    Love will find out the way.

William and Emily

EDGAR LEE MASTERS
(1869–1950)

There is something about Death
Like love itself!
If with some one with whom you have known
    passion,
And the glow of youthful love,
You also, after years of life
Together, feel the sinking of the fire,
And thus fade away together,
Gradually, faintly, delicately,
As it were in each other's arms,
Passing from the familiar room—
That is a power of unison between souls
Like love itself!

That Time of Year Thou Mayst in Me Behold

WILLIAM SHAKESPEARE

(1564–1616)

That time of year thou mayst in me behold,
When yellow leaves, or none, or few do hang
Upon those boughs which shake against the cold,
Bare ruin'd choirs, where late the sweet birds sang.
In me thou see'st the twilight of such day,
As after sunset fadeth in the west,
Which by and by black night doth take away,
Death's second self that seals up all in rest.
In me thou see'st the glowing of such fire,
That on the ashes of his youth doth lie,
As the death bed, whereon it must expire,
Consum'd with that which it was nourish'd by.
  This thou perceiv'st, which makes thy love more
    strong,
  To love that well, which thou must leave ere long.

Index of Titles

Index of Authors and Translators